under
the early morning trees

under
the early morning trees
poems

by Arnold Adoff   *illustrated by Ronald Himler*

E. P. Dutton   New York

Library of Congress Cataloging in Publication Data

Adoff, Arnold.   Under the early morning trees.

SUMMARY: A young girl enjoys a closeness with nature as
she roams through the strong old trees near her house.
1. Trees—Juvenile poetry. [1. Trees—Poetry.
2. Nature—Poetry] I. Himler, Ronald. II. Title.
PZ8.3.A233Un   811'.5'4   78-5561   ISBN: 0-525-41860-1

Published in the United States by E. P. Dutton, a Division
of Sequoia-Elsevier Publishing Company, Inc., New York

Published simultaneously in Canada by Clarke,
Irwin & Company Limited, Toronto and Vancouver

Editor: Ann Durell   Designer: Riki Levinson
Printed in the U.S.A.   First Edition
10 9 8 7 6 5 4 3 2 1

for
    ellen and
          ann
    jaime
         and
    leigh

there is a line of trees

      along the western side
of this old farm house
                where
all the weather blows

the trees are very old
            and very tall
and their branches are tipped
    with twigs and great
            green leaves
that brush the sky
and brush against
         the upstairs
bedroom window

the trees are a protection

      from the strong winds
and the hot sun
         and blizzard snows

and they move
and they
      shake
        and wake any one
who listens during
      sleep

the hundred hedge

      is what they always call it
and
      hundred hedge is what it
                 is

a hundred trees planted
a hundred
      years ago
in a line
      from the north
         most
point

      down the field
       to the south
         most
point
    of great
      grand pa$_s$ farm

she starts out   early and alone

      her eyes are open
      to the early morning
                  sky

      the stars are fading
and   the
        dipper falls
into
      the line of trees

               the sun begins to show

                  over the top branches
                of the cottonwood tree
           in the corner
           of the   field

                  like the tops of her high
                    and   shining boots
              through
                  the wet grass

she goes into the hedge each morning

to walk   and wake up walking
to eat   and feed the birds
and to
be alone

she wears blue pants tucked into
her high boots   and a yellow
jacket

she carries her pocket knife
inside
her left boot

she has a pair of cutting clippers
in her back pocket
and a soft
red
hat

under

    this hundred hedge
        is the   place
                    to be
    this hungry morning

    the osage branches
    stretch out an
                awning
    of frosted   leaves

over breakfast

on a special and flat
        rock

    two peaches
    in
      a sack

      a pack
of
    chocolate covered
           graham

      crackers

around

     her
       rock
black
    ants
       have
        work
for
the
day

this line of osage orange trees is tough

     against the winds   and heavy snows
but
     one young tree is wrapped
     in
       poison ivy vines
that wind
     around its branches

     pulling its branches
              down

she remembers not to touch the ivy vines

      but
           bends to the base of the tree
           and cuts the vine open
                     and
                    apart
        with her clippers

she wipes the clippers on the grass
and puts them back

and wipes her face

within the hedge

the elm are almost all gone
and
each spring another   few
leaf   out
and show
their
green   beginnings

then drop
their
leaves
and
die

they remain   like tan poles

among the green
trees
good places
for carving initials
and dates and   totem
faces
until the wind
wins
and breaks them
down

under the peeling bark

    the beetles and slugs
    and
       other hungry bugs
are
   marking their trails

and the redheaded
       wood
         pecker
is starting at the top

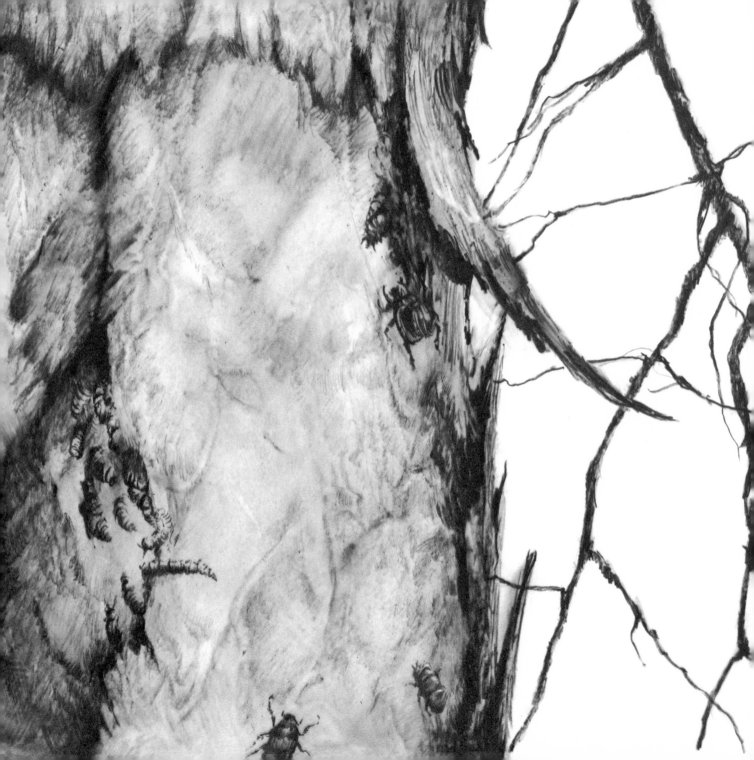

there is one

oak
for
two
    squirrels
and
one
    sycamore

      for
      blue

      jays

two

    blue
    wings
at
    top
of
    tree

    are
    free
      to fly
down
      for stale
      cracker

      jacks

red

bird
in
the

red
bud
tree

white
    pine
and
black
    walnut
and
blue
    spruce

white
    oak
and
wild
    cherry
and
blue
    berry

    sugar
    maple

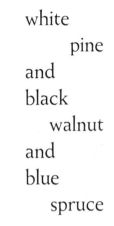

deep in the trees   are the noises

    of the birds   and footsteps

                              through dry leaves

the breeze is shaking the branches   but the
possum can only do
what
possums   do

               and runs
               and
                  climbs

she can be a possum   in the tree

to climb and hide

beside her long

pink

tail

and sit very still
and
shut her eyes
tight

become invisible

stepping into a perfect

    circle of violets

        and green

          onion

          grass

she has room to put one

        hand

between sharp thorns

six

   inches   long

hello

honey

locust

alone in the hedge   away from parents

    and brothers and friends
all
      names and places can be
      forgotten for a   while

there is time   to slide a knife
    along a sumac branch

sumac can be cut   and carved

      to make a pipe or walking stick
      the trick
            is in the peeling
             of the skin

long and thin
             in the open
                  sun
sumac
      has
      the
         palest
wood

under the deepest part   of the hedge

    she sees a mother quail   leading
    her chicks
            in a line

brown spiders are hanging
from their webs
            between the branches
            of forsythia and elm

and weaving the trees   together
    are wild grape and trumpet
                  vines
    climbing
        to the sun

the smallest baby

rabbit
    is lying on
some leaves
    by the
hollow
    tree

    very
      still
        and bent
          all
        wrong

she digs a deep hole

with a pointed stick
           and
puts the
      rabbit
        in
and
   picks
   some
      flowers

for
  a   blanket

    sleep
    good

in the high grass

        the
        cat
                who lives wild in the hedge
        has
                made
                        a
                nest
to
                have her kittens

at the south most point

of great
grand pa$_s$ farm

is the end of the
hedge

and at the end   is the barbed
wire
fence

at the edge

at the edge
are
corn
stalk
rows

and
rows

under the early morning trees

where they end
                    and the corn
                              field
                              begins
        are the sounds
                    of horses
        and new goats
                    and chickens
        from the neighbor farm

        this is   their time of day
                              and
        the roosters   are in their
                              power

and everybody s breakfast smells
        are
            under the breeze

the trees of the hedge

    and
    all things   of the
            hedge
    remain

will   remain   mothers and fathers
          until
the next morning   and
                      big

she knows that   brothers
                      are in their   places

                      calling names for
                                the
                      beginning day

                      they are calling
                          her
                      name

ARNOLD ADOFF moved from New York City to Yellow Springs, Ohio, years ago. For a long time he missed the stimulus of the city. But his work on *under the early morning trees* marked a turning point. "Each morning I would put on my long black boots, stick the clippers in my back pocket, and go out into the hedge." Each day brought him closer to the center of the hedge, closer to an understanding of his surroundings.

RONALD HIMLER illustrated two other books of poetry by Arnold Adoff: *TORNADO! POEMS* and *make a circle keep us in*. The numerous children's books he has illustrated include his own *Girl on the Yellow Giraffe,* and *Little Owl, Keeper of the Trees* which he wrote with his wife Ann. A graduate of the Cleveland Institute of Art, Mr. Himler lives in New York City.

The display was set in Weiss Roman foundry, and the text in Edelweiss Alphatype. The illustrations are one-color paintings on acetate. The book was printed by offset at Halliday Lithographers.